The Yorkshire Passport

BLUE EDITION

Official Tyke status is hereby bestowed upon:

____

This passport entitles the bearer on demand to pass peacefully into the environs of the greatest county on Earth, and to be afforded such assistance and protection as may be necessary.

I understand that by entering God's Own Country of Yorkshire, I am agreeing to abide by the following motto:

The Yorkshire Motto

'Ear all, see all, say nowt;
Eyt all, sup all, pay nowt;
And if iver tha does owt fer nowt –
Allus do it fer thissen.

Welcome to

God's Own Country

Le pays de Dieu
هسفن هللا دلب
El propio país de Dios
上帝的国家
O próprio país de Deus
भगवान का अपना देश
God's eigen land
Il paese di Dio
Guds eget land
Собственная страна Бога
神の国
Gottes eigenes Land
Τη χώρα του Θεού
własny kraj Boga
הארץ של אלוהים
Tír Dhí féin
Gwlad Duw ei hun

People's Republic of Yorkshire

The completely unofficial, 100% fake

PASSPORT

BLUE EDITION

FOR NOVELTY PURPOSES ONLY (OBVIOUSLY!)

Image credits

House of York Coat of Arms (p2): CC BY-SA 3.0; Judi Dench (p11): by Caroline Bonarde Ucci, CC BY 3.0; crown (p11): public domain; fish and chips (p15): public domain; teabags (p17): public domain; umbrella (p18): FreeImages.com/juri Staikov; mug of tea (p19): BSGStudio; boot (p20): 3lian.com; Yorkshire International Football Association crest (p24): by Yorkshire International Football Association, CC BY-SA 4.0; scroll (p31): zcool.com.cn; Yorkshire Flag (p33): public domain; wallet (p45): owattaphotos

All other images © Country Publications Ltd

Publisher information

First published in 2018 by Dalesman, an imprint of Country Publications Ltd
The Gatehouse, Skipton Castle, Skipton, North Yorkshire BD23 1AL
www.dalesman.co.uk

Reprinted 2019

ISBN 978-1-85568-371-6

Printed in China by Latitude Press.

Introduction

Since the first edition of this passport was published the calls for Yorkshire independence have only grown stronger.

There was even a debate in parliament about the possibility of "Yexit", and national newspapers carried headlines such as "Yorkshire plots devolution move" (*Express*) and "Could God's own county win control of its own fate?" (*Guardian*). The case was strengthened further in 2017 with the formation of the county's very own international football team (more of that later).

Then came the unrelated news that the UK's official passports would be turning blue. Like the official documents you take away on holiday, the original Yorkshire Passport had a red cover. Some folk didn't approve – it looked just a bit too Lancastrian.

Given that blue is the colour of the Yorkshire flag it does seem fitting that it should also be the colour of our passports.

So welcome to the new blue Yorkshire Passport. Enjoy the contents within – only please don't try and use it at passport control. They won't accept it. Yet!

What Yorkshire gave the world

Just about everything you can imagine actually originated in Yorkshire. Honestly.

Aeroplane

More than 100 years before the Wright brothers' first successful flight, George Caley of Brompton, near Scarborough, conceived the modern aeroplane as a fixed-wing flying machine with separate systems for lift, propulsion and control. He also constructed the first flying model aeroplane and designed the first glider to carry a man aloft.

Big Bang theory

The term "Big Bang", to describe the creation of all matter in the universe, was coined by Bingley astronomer Fred Hoyle in 1949.

Boomerang

You may think that the boomerang was invented in Australia but one historian believes it actually originated in Yorkshire. Terry Deary, author of the *Horrible Histories* series, says the Swastika Stone on Ilkley Moor is "the earliest representation of a boomerang. There's nothing else it could be".

Catseyes

Found down the middle of roads across the world, reflective roadstuds, were devised by Percy Shaw of Halifax in 1934. He is said to have invented them after the reflective eyes of a cat were caught in the beam of his car's headlamps, saving him from leaving the road.

Cement

The most common type of cement in use around the world, Portland cement is the basic ingredient of concrete, mortar and grout. It was pioneered by John Smeaton, of Austhorpe, Leeds, and as a result he is often known as "the father of civil engineering".

Christmas

It's believed the first time Christmas was celebrated in Britain was in York in 521AD.

Coca Cola

While the famous drink itself was not invented in Yorkshire, soda water, the basis for all fizzy drinks, was invented by Joseph Priestley of Birstall, West Yorkshire. Priestley also devised the first beer pump.

Computer memory

The Williams-Kilburn Tube, named after inventors Freddie Williams and Tom Kilburn was the first random-access digital storage device, better known as computer RAM. Kilburn, from Dewsbury, also jointly built the world's first computer that could store programs in electronic memory.

Diesel engine

The hot bulb engine, or heavy oil engine – the forerunner to the diesel engine – was invented by Halifax man Herbert Akroyd Stuart. So, although compression ignition oil engines have taken the name diesel after Rudolph Diesel, they could just as easily have been called akroyd engines.

Film

The world's first film was shot in Leeds by Louis Le Prince in 1888.

Flat-screen television

George Gray, a professor at the University of Hull, developed the molecules that made liquid crystal displays (LCDs) viable.

Football

The world's first football, club, Sheffield FC, was founded 24th October, 1857.

Hogmanay

Research suggests that

Hogmanay originated not in Scotland but Yorkshire. A household accounts ledger from Methley, Leeds, dating from 1443, contains the first recorded instance of the word "hogmanayse".

Lifeboat

Richmond-born Henry Greathead is credited with inventing the lifeboat in 1790. He built thirty-one boats which saved very many lives.

Linoleum

Lino flooring was created by Halifax-born Frederick Walton in 1855.

Pencil rubber

In 1770, Birstall inventor Joseph Priestley described a vegetable gum with the ability to rub out pencil marks. He called the substance "rubber".

Scratchy toilet paper

Ah, the memories! Who can ever forget the somewhat abrasive disinfectant-scented loo roll of our school days? This medicated tissue, often compared to tracing paper, was called Izal and was produced in Sheffield.

Spirograph

The fiendishly addictive geometric drawing toy, the spirograph, was developed by Leeds engineer Denys Fisher in 1965.

Yorkshire weather guide

January: Cowd

February: Reight Cowd

March: Proper cowd

April: Silin' it dahn

May: Still silin' it dahn

June: Nobbut middlin'

July: Fair ter middlin'

August: What's t' strange orange globe in t' sky?

September: Remember that sunny day?

October: Silin' it dahn again

November: Wuthering

December: Nithering

T' Yorkshire Cabinet

Yorkshire may have a flag, an anthem and its own language, but it doesn't yet have a head of state or a government. So here are our suggestions for the men and women to lead God's Own Country

Queen

Pride of York Judi Dench is surely the ideal choice to be Queen of Yorkshire. She's already a national treasure and as a Dame she's practically royalty already. Not only that but she's got form, having played Queen Victoria twice on the big screen, in 1997 and again in 2007, as well as taking on the role of Elizabeth I in *Shakespeare in Love*.

Prime Minister

Running a country is a bit like captaining a ship, so we've plumped for the greatest captain of all time. No, not Captain James Cook, but

Captain Jean-Luc Picard, captain of the starship USS Enterprise in *Star Trek: The Next Generation*. Okay, he's a fictional character but Picard, played with such authority by Mirfield legend Patrick Stewart, was a master of diplomacy and debate who was deeply moral, highly logical and intelligent. Surely all ideal traits in any Prime Minister.

Chancellor of the Exchequer

It goes without saying that the county's chancellor should be "prudent", i.e. good wi' brass. We've gone for Saltburn-born Chris Edwards. You may not know the name but this former Wakefield Market trader went on to establish Britain's thriftiest chain of shops, eventually opening 300 Poundworld stores before selling his stake in the business for £150 million. Turning £1 into £150m! Now that can't be bad!

Home Secretary

Who better to keep the crime rate down than Calderdale's finest, Sgt Catherine Cawood from *Happy Valley*? She's surely Britain's toughest cop.

Defence Secretary

Given that she regularly defeats the most evil baddies in the universe, Doctor Who herself, Jodie Whittaker, would be a grand choice as defence secretary. The Skelmanthorpe lass would keep the county safe through reputation alone.

Speaker of the House

Because Dewsbury-born Betty Boothroyd – the original and the best – has now retired, our suggestion would be Brian Blessed. With that booming voice, he's impossible to ignore so he'd be perfect at keeping those unruly politicians in check.

Foreign Secretary

Given that he's one of the world's most well-travelled men, could there be anyone more qualified than Sheffield-born Michael Palin? He's also been labelled Britain's nicest chap so he'd be ideal at negotiating with foreign despots.

Education Secretary

Jonny Mitchell, the no-nonsense former head of Dewsbury's Thornhill Community Academy, would prove popular. He certainly kept the bairns – and teachers – in check on the Channel 4's *Educating Yorkshire*.

Pensions Secretary

Given that he famously dies in just about every role

he plays, Sheffield star Sean Bean would be an interesting, if controversial, choice for Pensions Secretary. By keeping the death rate up, he'd certainly help to control the pensions deficit.

Transport Secretary

A man who definitely knows his cars is Doncaster lad Jeremy Clarkson. Jezza would certainly be outspoken, and he'd stick up for the county's petrolheads, though we fear cyclists and caravan owners would be given short shrift.

Health Secretary

For this key role we need somebody with an intimate knowledge of hospitals and all aspects of medicine. Who could be better, therefore, than Mr Bump? The accident-prone creation of Cleckheaton writer Roger Hargreaves would certainly bring vast experience of our healthcare system.

Minister for Food

As Yorkshire pudding is the food of the gods, it would make sense to select someone who knows their puds from their spuds. What better (or batter) choice, therefore, than Hull's own Aunt Bessie, the princess of puddings? The East Riding's baroness of batter somehow manages to conjure up 20 million Yorkshires every week. She must have strong arms!

Yorkshire vocabulary

Extend your Yorkshire vocabulary with our potted guide, including some common confusions made by Southerners

Ate

Eat. Not to be confused with the number eight, "summat ter ate" is a reference to a bag of chips, not the time of day.

Backend

Not, as you might assume a polite word for bottom, but the recognised term for autumn.

Badly

Not how your child's performing at school, rather a state of health. As in "How's Edna? Oh, she's badly".

Be reight

The universal response to all life's disasters, from grazing your knee to losing your job.

Blethering

Chatter among Southerners.

Brat

Someone else's child.

Brew

The answer to all life's problems.

Chuffed

Not something that steam engines do, but a state of euphoria experienced after getting an answer right on University Challenge.

Dry

As it's not a classification of weather we're overly familiar with in Yorkshire, the word here most often means thirsty. Because we nearly always are.

'Eckers like

Not likely, as in "Do I fancy a holiday in Blackpool? Do I 'eckers like."

Flippin' 'eck

Nothing to do with tossing pancakes, rather an exclamation of shock or surprise, as in, "Flippin' 'eck, there's that 'Arry Gration".

It's that man again...

T' lug oil

Lug oil

You may think this is a reference to carrying tubs of grease around, but in fact, it's the oddly-shaped thing on you shout into to get someone's attention.

Maftin'

A rarely used word in the Broad Acres, maftin' means hot or clammy. Usually reserved for holidays in Spain.

Mash

Nothing to do with potatoes; rather, what you should do with a teabag to make a decent brew.

Middlin'

The correct response to the question "How are you feeling?" whether you are glowing with health or dying of the plague.

Mi'sen

Myself, as in "Ah allus do mi best so Ah can nivver blame mi'sen for nowt".

Nithered

Given the bracing climate of Yorkshire, inhabitants have many words to describe the feeling you get when you step outside. This is one of them.

Mash 'em!

Nowt

Opposite of owt. As in "If there's owt for nowt, Ah'll be there with a barrow."

Radged

Less than impressed.

Silin'

Yorkshire folk have almost as many words to describe rain as the Eskimo have for snow. As in "It's silin' it dahn."

Summat

The highest standing it is possible for a Yorkshireman or woman to attain. As in "Ee is summat".

T'werk

Nothing to do with dancing. It's where Yorkshire people go each day between 9 and 5, as in "Tarra, love, Ah'm off t'werk."

The Yorkshire Survival Guide

Bit cowd – put t' kettle on

Fair jiggered – time fer tea

Forgot to Sky Plus Emmerdale – brew up

Lost thi car keys – cuppa

Feelin' badly – mash some tea

Got dumped – mek a brew

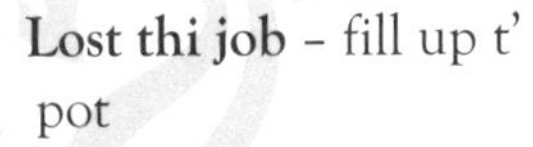

Lost thi job – fill up t' pot

Entire family drowned in a vat of Yorkshire pudding batter – it's time fer a proper brew

Out of teabags – duck and cover, the end of the world is nigh...

ARKENGARTHDALE
BOOZE
ARKENGARTHDALE
IDLE
WORKING
MEN'S CLUB
Booty
Lane
SELBY
KIPPAX
Blubberhouses
Harrogate
LAND OF
GREEN
GINGER
HULL

THE
SHAMBLES
YORK
Land
of
Nod
East
Yorkshire
NORTH YORK MOORS
FRYUP
NORTH YORK MOORS
Whip-Ma-Whop-Ma-Gate
Whip-Ma-Whop-Ma-Gate
YORK
Whip-Ma-Whop-Ma-Gate
YE OLDE
NAKED
MAN CAFE
SETTLE
North
Yorkshire
SEXHOW
North
Yorkshire

Yockenthwaite
WHARFEDALE
RIVER
FOULNESS
BEDLAM
HARROGATE
Jingling
Pot Cave
FANGFOSS
EAST RIDING
JUMP
South Yorkshire

RISE
HOLDERNESS
ARGUMENTS
YARD
Whitby
NEAR YORK
UGGLEBARNBY
NEAR YORK
CLECKHEATON
NUTTER
STREET
CRACKPOT
Swaledale
NORTHALLERTON
Thornton-le-Beans
NORTHALLERTON

Football's coming home

Every self-respecting country has its own football team, and now Yorkshire – birthplace of modern football – has an international side of its own.

Established in 2017, the Yorkshire International Football Association – nicknamed the Vikings – has become part of a global league that includes such giants as Tibet, Quebec, Greenland, Zanzibar, Darfur, South Ossetia and Northern Cyprus. Yorkshire played its inaugural match on Sunday 28th January at the 1,000-capacity Hemsworth Miners Welfare FC Community Club ground at Pontefract. The game against the Isle of Man ended in a respectable draw. Appropriately the sides ran out to the Yorkshire anthem On Ilkla Moor Baht 'At while children waved Yorkshire flags.

The Vikings wear a blue kit bearing the white rose of York and players must have been born within the historic county of Yorkshire.

"There is no voice internationally for Yorkshire, even through we're a significant region," said Yifa chairman Philip Hegarty. "As far as the outside world is concerned, we're just a subdivision of England, but of course we consider ourselves much more than that."

Not Yorkshire

Not Yorkshire

Yorks

BATTLE FOR DISPUTED BORDER TERRITORIES

DANGER ZONE

Beware of natives brandishing hotpots

Definitely not Yorkshire

Dah

Not Yorkshire

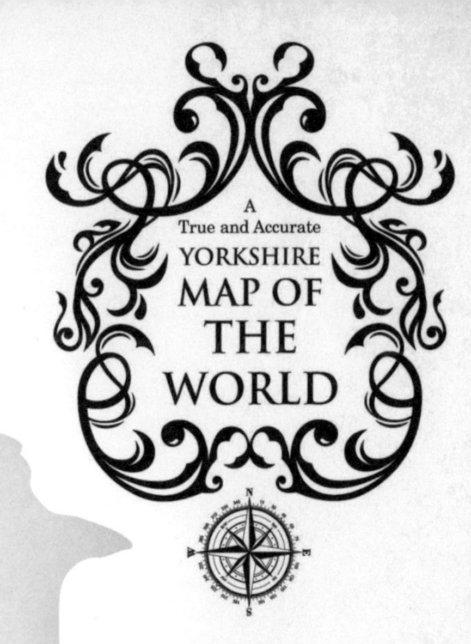

hire

Not Yorkshire

Not Yorkshire

arf

The Yorkshire anthem

Every country has its anthem and Yorkshire's is the rousing On Ilkla Moor Baht 'At (On Ilkley Moor without a hat).

Sung to the Methodist hymn tune Cranbrook, it is widely thought the song was composed by members of a Halifax church choir on an outing to Ilkley Moor.

The song is essentially a warning of the perils of being unsuitably dressed for the ravages of the Yorkshire climate.

First published in 1916, the song most likely originated during the latter half of the nineteenth century.

Arnold Kellett, author of *The Yorkshire Dictionary*, reports: "*Ilkla Mooar* came into being as a result of an incident that took place during a ramble and picnic on the moor. It is further generally believed that the ramblers were all on a chapel choir outing, from one of the towns in the industrial West Riding."

In 2013, Brian Blessed performed a rap on a new version of the anthem alongside opera singer Lesley Garrett.

In 2010 a competition was held to write a new anthem for the county. The winner of A Symphony for Yorkshire was Harrogate pensioner Doreen Brigham, who penned this stirring poem.

Sing a song of Yorkshire,
from the Humber to the Tees.
Of horses, wool and terriers,
of pudding and of cheese.
I know no other county
where the land is quite so fine.
England's lovely county. And
I'm proud to call it mine.

Where shining purple
heather stretches far across
the moor,
and the lapwing's cry above
me takes the place of traffic
roar.
And peace comes drifting
gently, there's no place
I'd rather be
than this land of hills and
valleys, from the Pennines to
the sea.

So when I've done my
roaming, and when my step
grows slow;
when heart and mind assure
me that the time has come
to go,
then let me rest in Yorkshire,
for it's there I want to lie
'neath sun and wind and
heather... and a gleaming
Yorkshire sky.

Yorkshire Day

Yorkshire Day takes place each year on the 1st August. Since it was first celebrated in 1975, it has grown into an internationally recognised event.

> The date was chosen as it was the day on which the Battle of Minden was fought

The day was established by the Yorkshire Ridings Society as a way of promoting the historic county of Yorkshire, which was divided up by local government reorganisation in 1974.

Each year, on Yorkshire Day, members of the society read a declaration of the integrity of Yorkshire at four of the Bars of York. A reading is held facing into each of the three Ridings and into the city.

The date was chosen as it was the day on which the Battle of Minden was fought, in recognition of the many Yorkshire soldiers who took part – many of them plucked roses from German gardens as they advanced to battle, and stuck them to their coats. 1st August was also the date of the abolition of slavery, a cause thanks in large part to the work of great Yorkshireman William Wilberforce.

The Yorkshire Day Pledge

I, (name), being a resident of the [West/North/East] Riding of Yorkshire [or City of York] declare:

That Yorkshire is three Ridings and the City of York, with these Boundaries of 1,145 years standing; That the address of all places in these Ridings is Yorkshire; That all persons born therein or resident therein and loyal to the Ridings are Yorkshiremen and women; That any person or corporate body which deliberately ignores or denies the aforementioned shall forfeit all claim to Yorkshire status.

These declarations made this Yorkshire Day [year]. God Save the Queen!

Yorkshire flag

These days the Yorkshire flag can be seen flying from hundreds of masts and poles across the county, but it is a relatively new invention.

The design was chosen from a shortlist of four

The design, featuring a white heraldic rose of York and a blue background, was only officially recognised as the flag of Yorkshire by the Flag Institute in 2008.

The successful registration of the design followed a request by the Yorkshire Ridings Society. Up until that point, although the flag had been in common usage since at least 1964, anyone daring to fly it without prior permission could have faced council prosecution.

The design was chosen from a shortlist of four, though other designs were not considered as they had no history of common use.

Amusingly, neighbouring Lancashire's flag – a red rose on a white background – was rejected by the Flag Institute because the Scottish town of Montrose had claimed it first. Instead, the red rose county had to go for what the *Guardian* called "a queasy combination of the red rose on a background field of bright yellow".

> **The flag had been in common usage since at least 1964**

The popularity of the Yorkshire flag soared with the arrival of the Tour de France in the county in 2014. Streets across the county were decked with versions large and small and many have remained in place ever since. There is surely now not another region in Britain where more flags are flown.

The Wit & Wisdom of Old Amos

With his pithy observations, curmudgeonly Yorkshireman Old Amos has been delighting and enlightening readers of *Dalesman*, the Yorkshire magazine, since 1953.

The very first Old Amos, left, was drawn by Rowland Lindup in 1953. Today, Old Amos is drawn by Rowland's son Peter (facing page)

The Yorkshire calendar

Your guide to celebrating Yorkshire all year round

JANUARY

Scorton Silver Arrow Tournament

The world's oldest recorded sporting event

FEBRUARY

Wakefield Rhubarb Festival

A celebration of Yorkshire's favourite vegetable

FEBRUARY

World Merrills Championships

Merrills is an ancient board game also known as Nine Men's Morris

FEBRUARY

Jorvik Viking Festival

The largest event of its kind in Europe, the annual festival is a celebration of York's Norse heritage

FEBRUARY

Shrove Tuesday

Yorkshire celebrations include the Ripon Pancake Race and Scarborough Skipping Day (see right)

FEBRUARY

Scarborough Skipping Day

The Shrove Tuesday celebration has taken place for around 100 years

MARCH/APRIL

Easter Sunday

Like Christmas and Hogmanay, a Yorkshire invention. The date of Easter was set at the Synod of Whitby in AD664

APRIL

World Coal Carrying Championships

Each year, men and women race through the streets of Gawthorpe carrying huge sacks of coal

APRIL

Mytholmroyd World Dock Pudding Competition

Dock Pudding is a local delicacy in the Calder Valley

31 JULY

Yorkshire Day Eve

When Yorkshire children hang up their trousers and excitedly await the arrival of the Yorkshire Day Ferret

1 AUGUST

Yorkshire Day

For Yorkshire folk this is like Christmas, but with more Yorkshire Pudding and fewer sprouts

2 AUGUST

Yorkshire Hangover Day

Pass t' Alka Seltzer, Doris, Ah've overdone it on t' Black Sheep...

27 NOVEMBER

Lancashire Day

Nothing to see here, move along...

NOVEMBER

Burning the Bartle

An ancient custom unique to West Witton, in which a stuffed figure is paraded and burnt

25 DECEMBER

Christmas Day

A Yorkshire invention – yes, seriously. The first secular Christmas is said to have been celebrated in York by King Arthur

31 DECEMBER

Hogmanay

Also a Yorkshire invention. The first recorded use of the word "hogmanayse" was in West Yorkshire in 1443

Yorkshire tea chart

Tha forgot t' teabag	Call that a brew?	Wrong
Wrong	Proper wrong	Nora's stockings
Mackintosh's toffee	Gettin' theer	That's moar like it
Builder's brew	Stick a spoon in me, Ah'm done	Out o' milk

Yorkshire Quotes

The Yorkshire dalesman is like many of the rivers among which he lives. He is slow but deep and, believe me, it takes years of constant touch with him before one can get into that happy position of being able to read him like a book. ('Wonten', Hawes, 1939)

Passion for one's country, yes in the very bones and heart of one, in one's writing, painting, poetry, the songs remembered on a lovely walk, the pictures formed for comfort in ugly places, the memory and tradition and love that makes a network to bind one's heart to the same grey windwept upland... My Heart's in Yorkshire. (Winifred Holtby)

For Angels treat her uplands
And Heaven's about her
downs
Her slumbering Wolds
a-gleaming
With little ancient towns.
From tale enchanted castle
To fairy-haunted glen:
There's witchery in Yorkshire
For Yorkshire-fostered men.
(D Violet Dinsdale, *Songs of Yorkshire*)

What do you think of Yorkshire Pudding, I'm frequently asked. Well, I've eaten this half a dozen times, and it has been a different size, shape and colour each time. I've had it with, without, under and above gravy, with and without meat. I am extremely confused. The whole thing is too mysterious. (Allan Eady, American visitor, 1966)

So pre-eminent in size over all the rest of the counties of England as to merit its name of the Land of Broad Acres, its boundaries marked for the most part by mountain stream and ocean, Yorkshire presents within itself perhaps the most complete epitome of physical geography and geological study to be found in any other equal area on the globe. (M Tait)

I rode over the mountains to Huddersfield. A wilder people I never saw in England; the men, women and children filled the streets as we rode along, and appeared just ready to devour us. (From the diaries of John Wesley)

Yorkshiremen are suspicious, obstinate, materialist, isolationist, nonconformist and blunt – and I like them as they are. (Bishop Eric Treacy)

...but he (the Yorkshireman) has many characteristics that are admirable and distinctly English: he has a dogged perseverance, great strength of will, sound judgement, ready wit. And withal he has a heart that is very tender. (W Riley, *A Yorkshire Suburb*, 1920)

I like my fellow men but there are times when it is wonderful to be utterly alone in a wide landscape. There aren't many places in England where you can do this, but you can do it in my Yorkshire. (James Herriot, AKA Alf Wight)

I've always been very proud of the fact I was born in Yorkshire because it's one of the few counties that has a very definable sense of itself. (Jeremy Paxman)

The Dales have never disappointed me. I still consider them the finest countryside in Britain, with their magnificent, clean and austere outlines of hill and moor, their charming villages and remote whitewashed farms, their astonishing variety of aspect and appeal, from the high gaunt rocks down to the twinkling rivers. (JB Priestley)

The Yorkshireman has, no doubt, a way of speaking his mind very freely, and telling you what he thinks. However unpleasant this habit may be at times, it has its advantages; you at least know where you are with them and you can always tell whether a Yorkshireman likes or dislikes what you do – he as good as tells you. (*Yorkshire Folk-Talk*, 1892)

Yorkshire is much the biggest county in England, indeed clearly a "country", a diverse geographical entity of great cities, ancient cathedrals, industrial estates, seats of learning, wild uplands and sweeping coasts. Its natural landscape is as varied as any in Europe, from the raw limestone of Pennines to the spreading Vale of York, from the lush Dales to the bare Cleveland Hills. (Simon Jenkins)

How rich is our county in rivers; in little dales and mighty dales; in crumbling castles, in abbeys and priories; in inns and sturdy villages; in scrambling walls and rugged roads; in boulders, screes and scars; in noble halls and pleasances; in lonely tarns, in moor and mountain, in wild birds, in tumbling ghylls, in gnarled oaks and ash and thorns, in firs and pines; in generous food; in lusty lads and lasses; in short – for my breath fails me – in every decent thing the heart of man could desire. (Alfred J Brown)

It's absolutely impossible for any of us, no matter how fond we may be of our native county, to comprehend its vast size. Folks who live outside the borders cannot form any conception of its enormous area, of the difference between its three Ridings, of the alternations in scenery, of the gulf which separates the men of its town and cities from men of the lovely dales and woodlands. (JS Fletcher)

Lesser-spotted
Yorkshireman's Wallet

(Extremum tightus blokeia)

Only a privileged few have been lucky enough to catch a glimpse of this elusive beast and as a result very little is known about it.

Its habitat tends to be the dark recesses of a murky, little-visited region known as "Yorkshireman's Pocket" and once it has made its nest here, the wallet rarely, if ever, emerges.

It has been observed that you can entice the wallet from its lair by shouting key phrases such as "It's your round" or "Has thi got any spare change?" although the wallet only emerges for a fleeting second, only to return almost immediately to its dark hiding place.

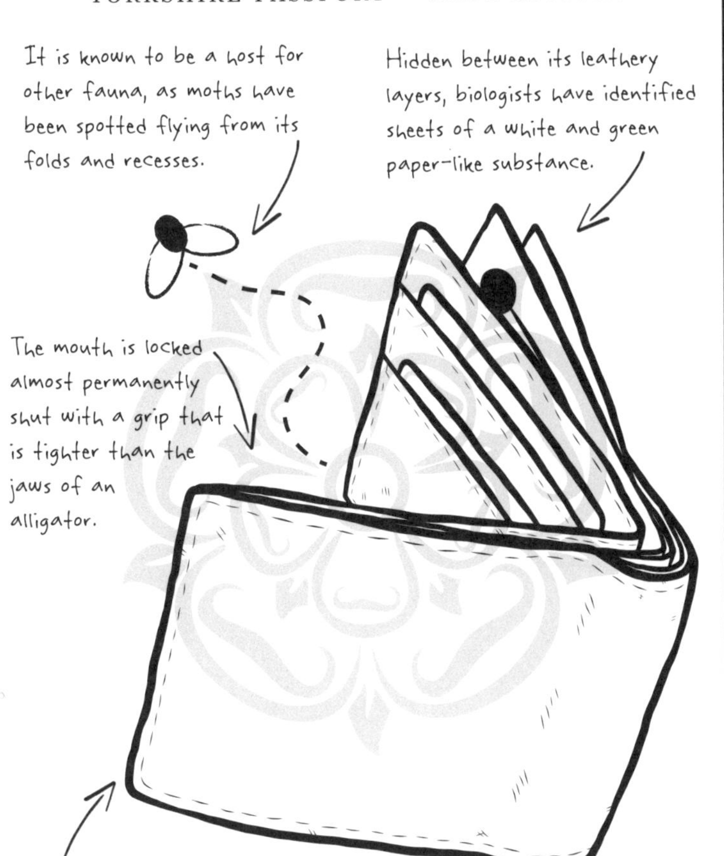

Generally brown in colour, the wallet appears to have a leathery skin.

It is not known what the wallet feeds on though there is speculation that it devours metal spheres.

Yorkshire Insults

Yorkshire	English
Yer daft apeth	You're something of a fool but I like you nonetheless
By 'eck, ee's a barmpot	I say, he is rather an idiot
Yer a dozy twonk	You're not the brightest button in the box
'Ow do, buggerlugs	Hello there, you old grump
A daft wazzock	An utter nincompoop
Tha's a mardy bum	You're awfully grumpy
Tha's black bright	You are decidedly dirty
She's fair clarted	She's wearing rather a lot of make-up

E's proper cack-'anded	He's somewhat clumsy
Tha meks a better door than a winder	Would you mind awfully moving aside, I can't see the television
Yer reight nesh	You're decidedly soft – it's not that cold
'E's neither use nor ornament	That chap is perhaps not the most capable
Tha's not so green as tha's cabbage-lookin'	Congratulations, you are not as stupid as you appear
'E's soft in t' 'ead	That gentleman is not very clever
Get ower thissen	Please prevail from being so conceited and un-Yorkshirelike
Think on	Watch yourself

Supwier?	What on earth is her problem?
It's like Blackpool bloody illuminations in 'ere	You have irresponsibly left one solitary lightbulb switched on
There's nowt so queer as folk	People – particularly those not from Yorkshire – are decidedly odd
That's rank	That hotpot is rather disagreeable
Shut tha cake 'oil	Would you mind awfully turning down the volume
Tha reeks!	You smell somewhat unsavoury